W9-CPP-620

Cool STUFF — for — FAMILY & FRIENDS

A Division of ABDO

ABDO
Publishing Company

PAM SCHEUNEMANN

visit us at www.abdopublishing.com

Published by ABDO Publishing Company, a division of ABDO, P.O. Box 398166, Minneapolis, Minnesota 55439. Copyright © 2012 by Abdo Consulting Group, Inc. International copyrights reserved in all countries. No part of this book may be reproduced in any form without written permission from the publisher. Checkerboard Library™ is a trademark and logo of ABDO Publishing Company.

Printed in the United States of America, North Mankato, Minnesota
052011
092011

 PRINTED ON RECYCLED PAPER

Design and Production: Mighty Media, Inc.
Series Editors: Katherine Hengel and Liz Salzmann
Photo Credits: Anders Hanson, Shutterstock

The following manufacturers/names appearing in this book are trademarks:
3M™ , Aleene's® Tacky Glue®, Americana® Multi-Purpose™ Sealer, Craft Smart™, Crafter's Pick™, Creative Imaginations®, Heat n Bond®, PearlEx®, Rubber Stampede™, Sculpey®, Westcott™

Library of Congress Cataloging-in-Publication Data
Scheunemann, Pam, 1955-
  Cool stuff for family & friends : creative handmade projects for kids / Pam Scheunemann.
     p. cm. -- (Cool stuff)
  Includes index.
  ISBN 978-1-61714-981-8
  1. Handicraft--Juvenile literature. I. Title.
  TT160.S2967 2012
  745.5--dc22
                        2011003045

CONTENTS

HANDMADE GIFTS

FROM THE

There's nothing like giving a **handmade** gift. Handmade gifts are special. Your family and friends will appreciate all the time and creativity that you put into the project. This makes gift giving all the more fun!

Handmade gifts can be **customized**. You're the creator, so you can make it unique! Think about the person that will receive the gift. Use his or her favorite colors! Think about the person's interests too. If you know what people like, it's easy to make gifts they'll love!

HEART

Permission & Safety

- Always get permission before making any type of craft at home.
- Ask if you can use the tools and supplies needed.
- If you'd like to do something by yourself, say so. Just make sure you can do it safely.
- Ask for help when needed.
- Be careful when using knives, scissors, or other sharp objects.
- Have an adult help you use an iron or an oven.

Be Prepared

- Read the entire activity before you begin.
- Make sure you have all the tools and **materials** listed.
- Do you have enough time to complete the project?
- Keep your work area clean and **organized**.
- Follow the directions for each activity.
- Clean up after you are finished for the day.

TOOLS AND

CORK SHEET

FELT

WOMEN'S TIGHTS

CHENILLE STEMS

DOUBLE-SIDED IRON-ON ADHESIVE

FABRIC GLUE

RIBBONS

ALUMINUM FOIL

CRAFT FOAM

DECORATIVE BRADS

POLYMER CLAY

PILLAR CANDLES

MATERIALS

METALLIC PIGMENT POWDER

HEMP

LOBSTER CLASPS

ALPHABET STICKERS

FOAM BRUSHES

RUBBER STAMPS

PAPER PUNCH

FABRICS

SANDPAPER

WOODEN SKEWERS

ACRYLIC SEALER

ACRYLIC PAINTS

MOUSE PAD

STUFF YOU'LL NEED

1 SHEET OF NATURAL CORK   FABRIC
PEN   IRON
SCISSORS   BOOKS
DOUBLE-SIDED, IRON-ON ADHESIVE

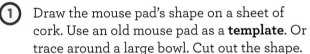

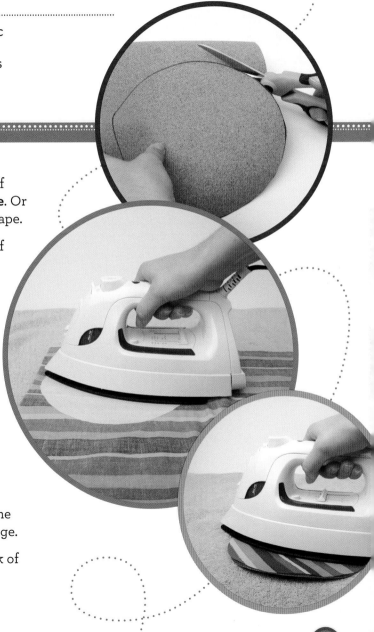

1. Draw the mouse pad's shape on a sheet of cork. Use an old mouse pad as a **template**. Or trace around a large bowl. Cut out the shape.

2. Place the cork cutout on the paper side of some iron-on **adhesive**. Trace and cut out the shape.

3. On a protected surface, iron the fabric. Place it face down.

4. **Fuse** the iron-on adhesive to the fabric with an iron. Follow the directions on the iron-on adhesive package.

5. Cut the shape out of the fused fabric. Place the fabric on the cork to make sure it's a good fit. Trim if needed.

6. Remove the backing from the iron-on adhesive and fuse it to the cork. Follow the directions on the iron-on adhesive package.

7. Put the finished mouse pad under a stack of books until the adhesive cools.

DRAFT DODGER

STUFF YOU'LL NEED

WOMEN'S TIGHTS

SCISSORS

PAPER

MASKING TAPE

KITTY LITTER OR SAND

CUP

PAPER TOWEL TUBE

CHENILLE STEMS

PENCIL

POM-POMS

FABRIC GLUE

FELT

GOOGLY EYES

1 Cut one of the legs off of the tights.

2 Form a funnel with a piece of paper. Put the narrow end into the paper towel tube. Tape it in place. Put the paper towel tube halfway in the leg.

3 Fill the leg with kitty litter. Fill it until it is long enough to go across the bottom of a door.

4 Press the kitty litter inside the stocking. It should be packed in tightly. Squeeze the end to make the head part a bit larger than the body.

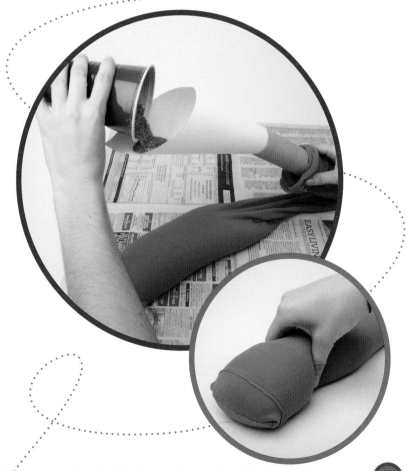

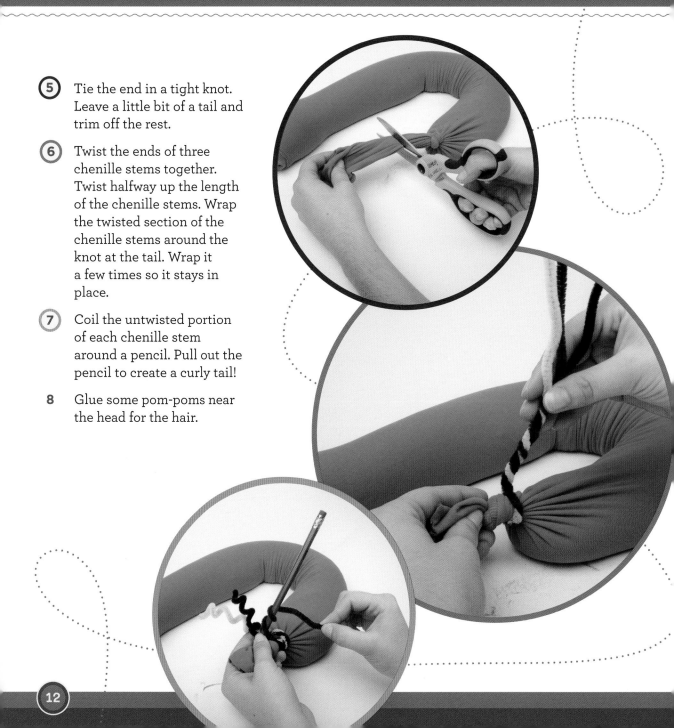

(5) Tie the end in a tight knot. Leave a little bit of a tail and trim off the rest.

(6) Twist the ends of three chenille stems together. Twist halfway up the length of the chenille stems. Wrap the twisted section of the chenille stems around the knot at the tail. Wrap it a few times so it stays in place.

(7) Coil the untwisted portion of each chenille stem around a pencil. Pull out the pencil to create a curly tail!

8 Glue some pom-poms near the head for the hair.

9. Cut out some felt shapes. You'll need ears, a nose, and a tongue. Cut out a circle to go behind each googly eye. Does your draft dodger need some spots? Cut those out too!

10. Glue on the felt pieces. Only glue half of each ear. That way they'll stand up!

11. Glue on the googly eyes.

12. For antennae, make two chenille stem coils. Leave a bit of the stem uncoiled at the ends. Put one behind each ear. Stick the uncoiled ends into the head, then back out about 1 inch (3 cm) away. Twist each end around its stem so the antennae stay in place.

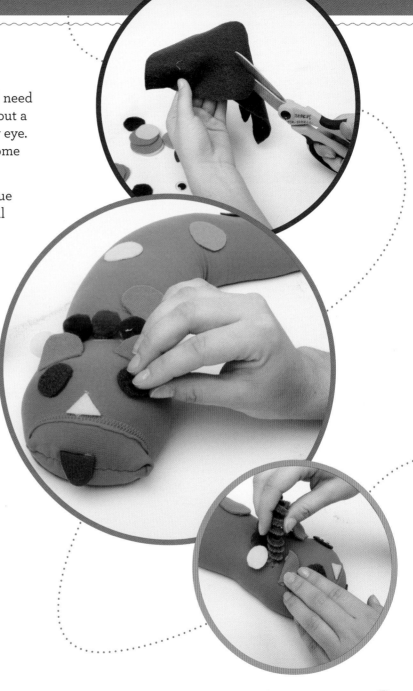

TIP

The draft dodger can curl up in a corner when not in use.

HAMMER TIME

THIS IS A PERFECT GIFT FOR ANY ADULT!

STUFF YOU'LL NEED

NEWSPAPER
PLAIN PAPER
PENCIL
WOOD-HANDLED HAMMER
SANDPAPER

PAPER TOWEL
ACRYLIC PAINTS
FOAM & PAINT BRUSHES
FINE TIP MARKER
ACRYLIC SEALER

1. Cover your work area with newspaper. On a piece of plain paper, trace around the hammer handle. Create several tracings of the handle so you can practice your **designs** on them later. Set them aside.

2. **Sand** the wooden handle of the hammer. This prepares it for painting.

3. Wipe the handle down with a damp paper towel to remove the sanding dust. Let the handle dry.

4. Get rid of the newspaper with the sanding dust. Put down fresh newspaper.

5. Paint one side of the handle white. Let it dry before painting the other side. If needed, use 2 coats. Let the paint dry.

6. While the paint dries, plan your **design**. Use the person's name or initials. Make sure you have enough room for the letters. Draw the other designs you want on the handle.

7. Choose a background color for the handle. Light colors work well. You'll be able to see your pencil marks on the handle later. Paint one side of the handle. Let it dry before painting the other side.

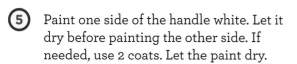

TIP

Be prepared to do a little waiting during this project. There are many layers of paint. It is important to let the paint dry before moving on to the next step.

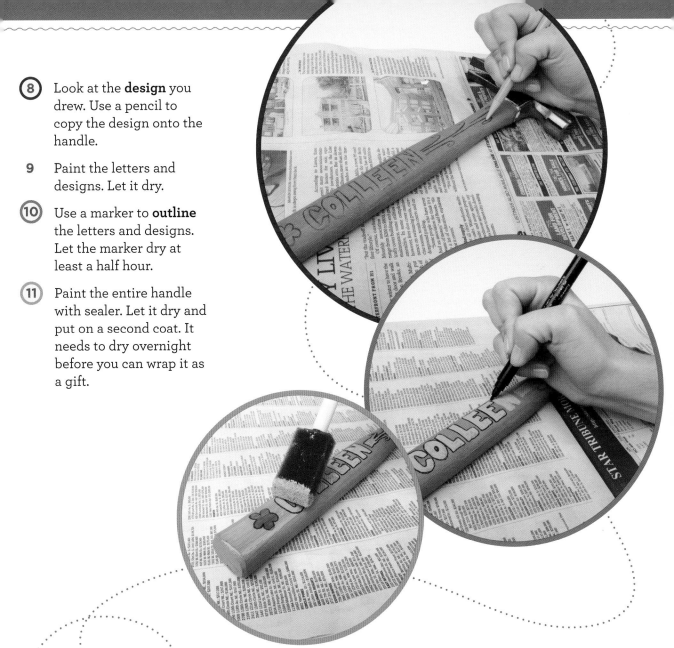

8. Look at the **design** you drew. Use a pencil to copy the design onto the handle.

9. Paint the letters and designs. Let it dry.

10. Use a marker to **outline** the letters and designs. Let the marker dry at least a half hour.

11. Paint the entire handle with sealer. Let it dry and put on a second coat. It needs to dry overnight before you can wrap it as a gift.

Cool
COASTERS

NEWSPAPER
RULER
PENCIL
CRAFT FOAM

SCISSORS
PAPER PUNCH
GLUE
FOAM BRUSH

DECORATIVE GEMS (OPTIONAL)
HOT GLUE GUN (OPTIONAL)

CUT OUT COASTERS

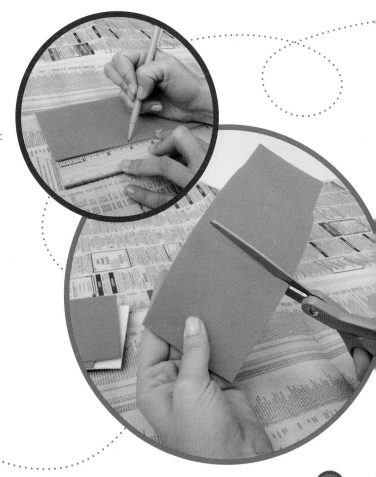

1. Cover your work area with newspaper. Using a ruler and pencil, draw a square on craft foam. Cut out the square.

2. Trace the square onto a second piece of craft foam. It should be a different color than the first. One square is the bottom, and one is the top.

3. Use a paper punch to make a pattern on the top piece of craft foam.

4. Use a foam brush to apply a thin layer of glue to the back side of the top piece.

5. Place the top onto the bottom piece and press together. Wipe off any extra glue.

VARIATION

Make the top piece of foam smaller than the bottom piece. Glue gems around the edge!

SUPER SPIRAL COASTERS

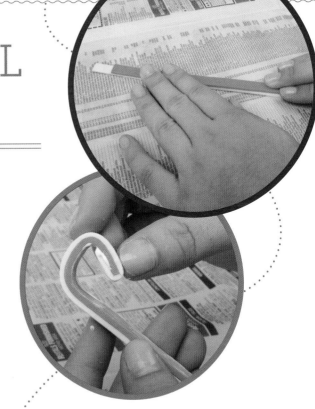

1   Cut out two ¼-inch (1 cm) wide strips of craft foam. Each should be a different color.

2   Make one strip ½ inch (2 cm) longer than the other. Coat one side of the shorter strip with glue. Press the strips together.

3   Glue the longer, bottom piece up onto the shorter piece. Apply glue along the rest of the shorter piece. Tightly roll up the strips to form a spiral. Flatten it out on a table as it dries. To increase the coaster size, add more strips of both colors.

VARIATION

Make different sized spirals and glue them together. You may need to use hot glue. Ask an adult to help you.

NECKLACE

THIS QUICK PROJECT MAKES A GREAT GIFT FOR ANYONE!

STUFF YOU'LL NEED

POLYMER CLAY
WAX PAPER
TAPE
SMOOTH-SIDED GLASS JAR
RUBBER STAMP

CRAFT KNIFE
WOODEN SKEWER
ALUMINUM FOIL
METALLIC PIGMENT POWDER
OVEN

COTTON SWAB
HEMP
SCISSORS
MEDIUM-SIZED BEAD

(1) **Knead** the polymer clay until it is smooth. Tape a piece of wax paper onto your work surface. Using a jar, roll the clay into a sheet that is ¼-inch (1 cm) thick.

(2) Center a rubber stamp on the clay. Use a jar to firmly press the stamp into the clay.

(3) Use a craft knife to cut out the **pendant**.

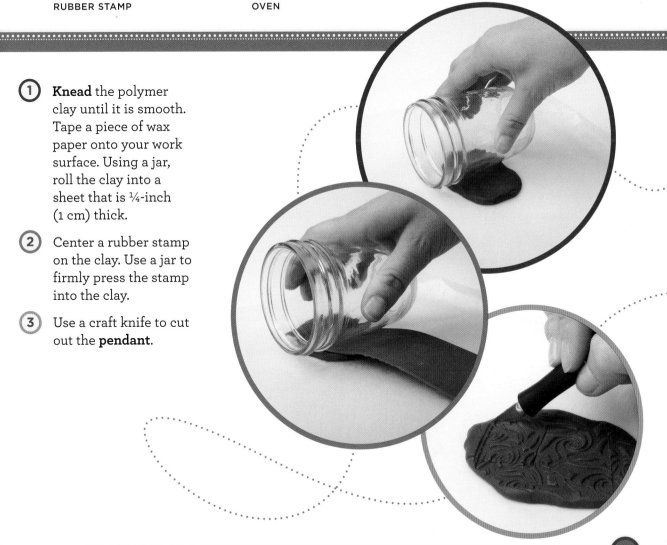

4. Gently twist a wooden skewer through the top of the **pendant** to make a hole. Don't touch the stamp pattern.

5. Place the pendant on aluminum foil. With a cotton swab, apply metallic pigment onto the stamp pattern.

6. Bake the pendant on the foil. Follow the directions on the polymer clay package. Let it cool, then carefully wipe off any **excess** metallic powder.

7. Cut a piece of hemp 36 inches (91 cm) long. Push the hemp through the hole in the pendant. Pull through until there's an even amount on each side.

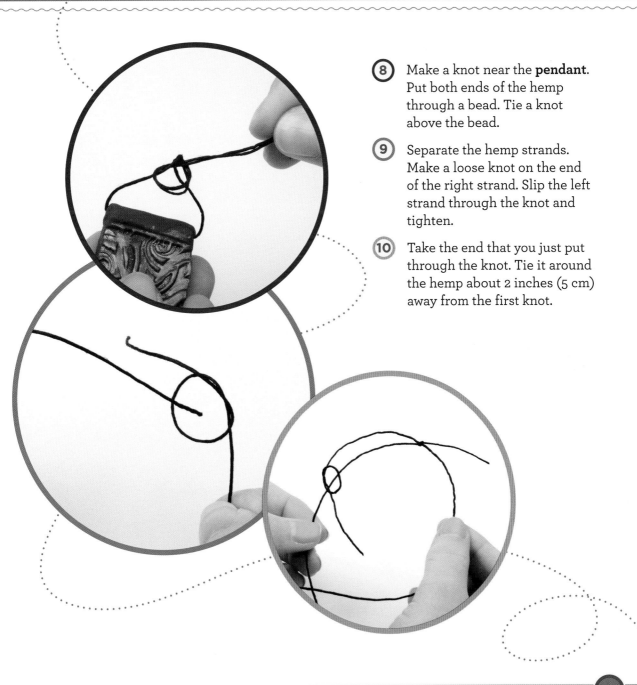

8. Make a knot near the **pendant**. Put both ends of the hemp through a bead. Tie a knot above the bead.

9. Separate the hemp strands. Make a loose knot on the end of the right strand. Slip the left strand through the knot and tighten.

10. Take the end that you just put through the knot. Tie it around the hemp about 2 inches (5 cm) away from the first knot.

Stroke Counter

GOLF GIFT

THIS GIFT WILL SUIT ANY GOLFER TO A TEE!

STUFF YOU'LL NEED

SCISSORS   LOBSTER CLASP, 29 MM
HEMP   12 BIG BEADS
RULER   2 SMALL BEADS

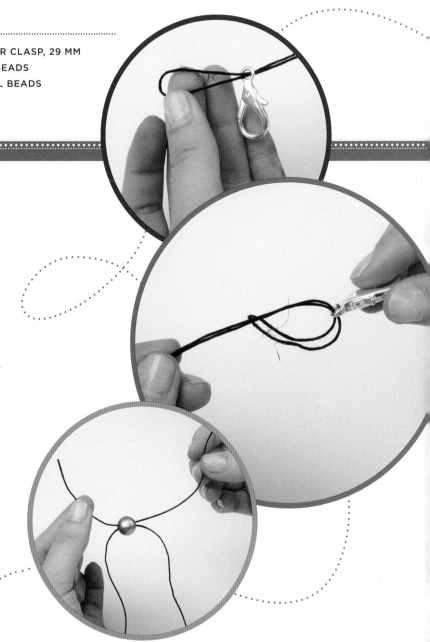

1. Cut the hemp to 24 inches (61 cm). Fold the hemp in half. Put the loop through the ring on the lobster clasp.

2. Pull the hemp ends through the loop. This ties the hemp to the lobster clasp.

3. To string the beads, put the hemp ends through a bead from opposite sides.

4. Repeat using all 12 beads. Tie the ends together. Leave 1 inch (3 cm) between the last bead and the knot.

5. Put both ends through a small bead. Tie a double-knot to hold the bead in place. Trim the extra hemp.

CANDLES

THIS IS A SUPER QUICK WAY TO MAKE A PERSONAL GIFT!

STUFF YOU'LL NEED

3 PILLAR CANDLES
WIDE RIBBON
NARROW RIBBON
SCISSORS
GLUE

DECORATIVE BRADS
ALPHABET STICKERS
DECORATIVE GEMS
STICKERS

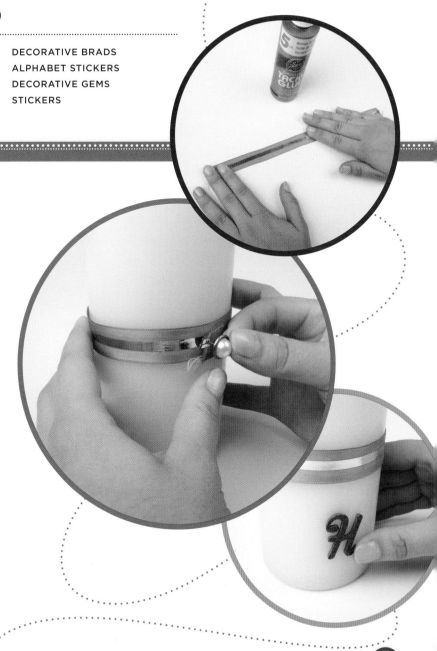

1   Cut a narrow ribbon so it is
    1 inch (3 cm) longer than
    the candle is around. Cut
    a wide ribbon to the same
    length.

2   Glue the narrow ribbon
    in the center of the wide
    ribbon.

3   Wrap the ribbon set around
    the candle. Fold under one
    end. Use a decorative brad
    to hold the ribbon in place.

4   Add an alphabet sticker.
    Use the first letter of the
    person's first name.

5   Repeat on the other two
    candles. Use the initials
    from the person's middle
    and last names. Decorate
    the candles with gems and
    stickers! Add a bit of glue to
    the stickers if needed.

CONCLUSION

The projects in this book are **designed** to inspire your creativity! Think about the people for whom you are making the gifts. What will they like? The more you **customize** a gift, the more special it becomes.

Go a step further. Do some **research**! Try different variations and **materials**. See what you have around the house. Be creative. The sky is the limit!

GLOSSARY

adhesive – a substance like glue that sticks things together.

customize – to make or fit something to one person's needs.

design – a decorative pattern.

fuse – to use heat to join two things together.

handmade – made by hand instead of made by a machine.

knead – to press, fold, and stretch something, such as bread dough.

material – the substance or substances of which something is made.

organize – to arrange things neatly and in order.

outline – to draw around the edge of something.

pendant – a hanging ornament, especially on a necklace.

research – the act of finding out more about something.

sand – to smooth something with sandpaper.

template – a shape or pattern that you draw or cut around to make the same shape on another piece of paper or other material.

Web Sites

To learn more about cool stuff, visit ABDO Publishing Company on the World Wide Web at www.abdopublishing.com. Web sites about cool stuff are featured on our Book Links page. These links are routinely monitored and updated to provide the most current information available.

INDEX